Sunset
Remodeling Ide
More Living Space

By the Editors of Sunset Books and Sunset Magazine

Lane Publishing Co. • Menlo Park, California

Book Editor
Cynthia Overbeck Bix

Coordinating Editor
Suzanne Normand Mathison

Design
Kathy Avanzino Barone
Steve Reinisch

Illustrations
Mark Pechenik
Rik Olson
Bill Oetinger
Clyde Foles
Stephanie Reed

When you need a little more space . . .

Most of us have imagined at one time or another our "dream" house—the perfect home, with room for everyone and everything in our lives. Perhaps your present house fulfilled many of these dreams when you first moved in. But lately, you're beginning to wake up to some nagging realities—a lack of space for your new interests, closets that overflow with your possessions, cramped, dark rooms where you yearn for light and space.

You could embark on the time-consuming, frustrating, and often expensive search for a new house. But that may not be necessary. Why not remake the house you have now into the house of your dreams?

Where to begin? Right here, with this book. Browse through our enticing gallery of remodeling ideas for inspiration. You'll find all kinds of space-expanding solutions, from raised ceilings to "pushed-out" walls, from one-room additions to multistory renovations, along with case histories of each project. Among all these exciting possibilities, there's certain to be one idea that's right for you.

Read, think, and imagine. Then consult the back of the book for practical advice on planning and managing a remodeling project of any size.

Your own house may turn out to be your dream house after all!

We extend special thanks to Fran Feldman for her thorough editing of the manuscript.

Cover: An addition to a charming old farmhouse, this airy porch provides a haven of peacefulness and repose all year round. Additional photos and description appear on pages 48–49. Architect: Lyndon/Buchanan Associates. Photograph by Glenn Christiansen. Cover design by Williams & Ziller.

Editor, Sunset Books: David E. Clark

First printing April 1986

CONTENTS

SPECIAL FEATURES

Bold addition oriented to lakefront life style

From beach cottage to year-round house

Addition to this beach house enhanced its livability and provided an entire new wing, including studio, mudroom, and decks.

This house, which began as a beach cottage, was small and dark, and had a tight, closed-in feeling. Located on a lake close to town, it was worth remodeling for family living.

Leaving the small living room and dining room intact, the addition created a new family area off the kitchen. Relocation of the house's entry improved traffic patterns, greatly increasing the effective area of the original living room. Oriented to beach activities, the addition had to provide plenty of storage space for boating and camping gear, as well as a pottery studio, mud room, and half bath.

The new addition has two floors. Downstairs are the family room, studio, half bath, and mud room. Upstairs are a sewing room, the master bedroom, and a bathroom. Higher ceilings, as well as doors and windows opening out to the beach, provide the open, light, spacious feeling the owners wanted.

The small size and low ceilings of the original house created a problem in blending old and new. But lapping the roof of the addition over the original house to form a clerestory above the stairwell tied the two structures together esthetically. Also, windows in the addition were scaled to the original house, and the first-floor roof overhangs the deck and entry.

Architect: Carolyn D. Geise.

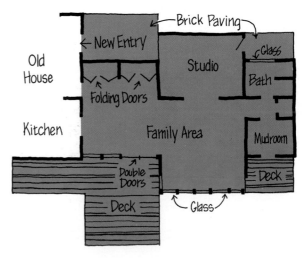

Window wall *faces the beach. With its wood-shingled exterior and simple lines, house blends into its environment.*

Two-story addition yields breakfast room, downstairs pantry

Upstairs, master bedroom gains walk-in closet

The owners of this house didn't feel comfortable having all their meals in the dining room. They wanted a small, informal area off the kitchen for breakfasts and for storage. And they wanted more closet space upstairs off the master bedroom. They answered their needs with a simple, unobtrusive two-story addition.

The addition blends in splendidly with the existing house, echoing its forms and materials. Since the breakfast room backs onto a hill, the owners wanted a view up as well as out; consequently, a tempered glass roof offers uphill views to azaleas and pines. And an upstairs skylight illuminates the new walk-in closet and dressing room.

It's a small addition. The downstairs portion, connected to the kitchen by an open doorway, is 7½ by 12½ feet. Two-thirds of this space is eating area; the rest is pantry and broom closet. In cool weather, air near the glass is warmed by an energy-saving draft barrier heater on a small ledge at the base of the windows.

Architect: Donald King Loomis.

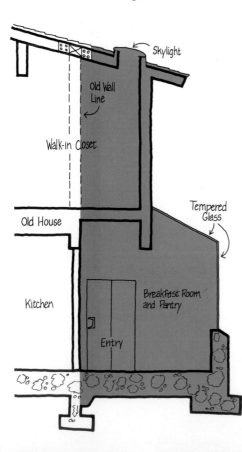

Small addition makes a big difference. Slanted glass roof, glass wall let in plenty of light. New breakfast room downstairs and walk-in closet upstairs merge perfectly with existing house.

Bland turned beautiful

Space between house and carport becomes new entry, bedroom, study

When the owners of this house first bought it, it was, in their words, "nondescript, but in a good location." They wanted something they could do a lot with.

Their addition wrought dramatic changes in the 40-year-old structure, situated on a narrow lot. Between the old house and the old carport they built a tall wooden box, windowless to the street, containing a new entry, bedroom, and study. The addition's bare, street-side façade hides the old structure and gives privacy. It also deliberately conceals what's inside — a varied collection of plants, rugs, contemporary furniture, and small artifacts that fills every room.

The new entry corridor, with high, skylight ceiling, leads past rows of plants to the old entry hall — now the central hub of the house. Here the wall opening between the old entry and the living room was enlarged.

The small, square study addition has a skylight along one side. From the study, a stairwell against the facade wall leads upstairs to the tall new bedroom.

The new interior spaces have an interesting and varied feel because of different sizes, ceiling heights, and window placements. Openings between rooms were enlarged to give contrastingly deep views from one room into another and to the outdoors. For instance, it's about 55 feet from the front door to the window wall at the rear of the house; the view from the entry extends through three rooms.

Architect: William Turnbull, MLTW/Turnbull Associates.

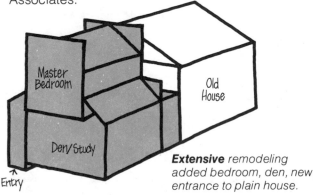

Extensive remodeling added bedroom, den, new entrance to plain house.

Second-story skylight

Acrylic roof panels

Above: At entrance to den and study, second-story skylight illuminates display shelves. *Below:* Windowless façade ensures privacy from street.

TEN OPTIONS: Ways a house can grow

Gaining extra living space in your home may involve anything from knocking down one interior wall to building a large addition. How you choose to add or open up space depends on a variety of factors—your family's living patterns, your budget, your home's present layout, and more.

The drawings below and on the facing page show a range of space-expanding options. All of these ideas, along with examples of actual additions, conversions, and other remodels, are explored throughout this book.

Analyzing your options

When you first begin to think about expanding your living space, it's important to analyze exactly how your present house fails to meet your needs. Do the rooms feel cramped, lacking easy flow? Perhaps some rooms are underutilized, some overcrowded with activity. Could a rearrangement of your existing space provide extra elbow room? Or is what you really need a new family room, an extra bedroom or bath, or more storage space?

Once you know what you need, explore a wide variety of options on paper. Don't settle for the first or most obvious plan until you've considered many alternatives.

If you opt for an addition, there are lots of exciting possibilities. You can go up, down, or sideways—add a second story or basement, build on a one or two-story addition, or extend the front, back, or side of the house.

Alternative strategies

If your budget or your needs don't call for a major remodel or addition, consider other ways to add or open up space. Sometimes, just raising a ceiling can make a dark, cramped room feel less confining. Or think about tearing down a wall between two small rooms to open up the space you already have. Perhaps you need just a few extra feet of new space—for a walk-in closet in the bedroom or a breakfast nook off the kitchen. If so, "push out" a wall to create a pop-out.

Finally, take a fresh look at unused or underused areas in your house. An attic, basement, or garage, or even a little-used porch can often be transformed into bright, livable space.

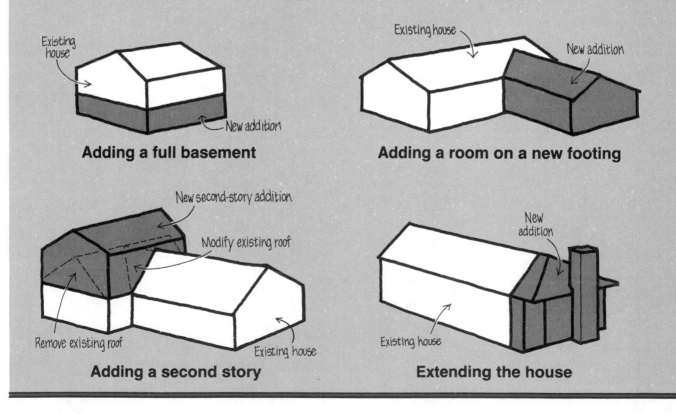

Adding a full basement

Adding a room on a new footing

Adding a second story

Extending the house

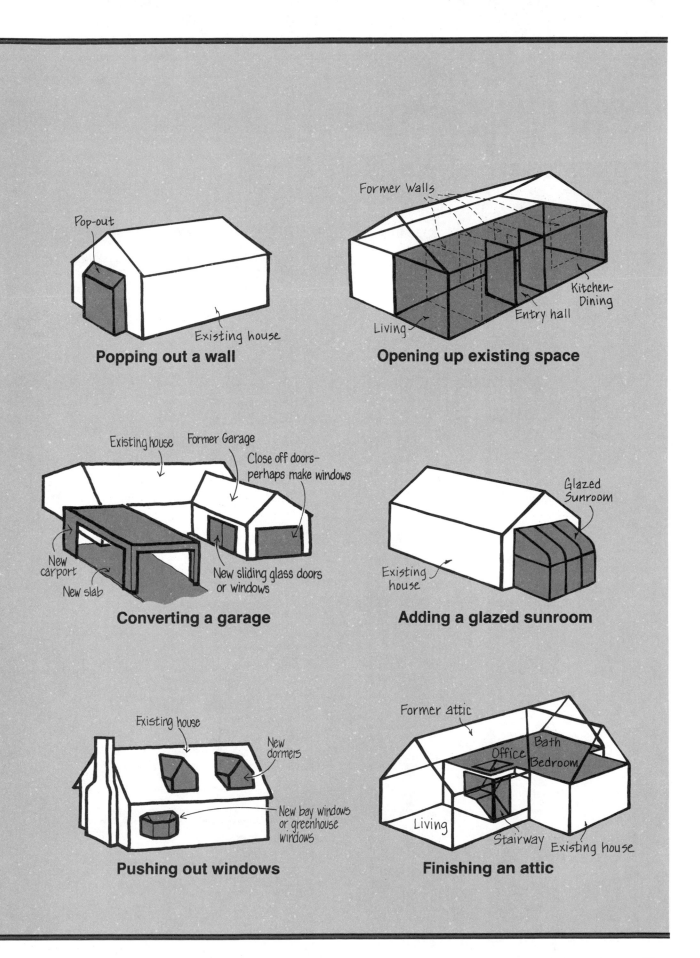

Popping out a wall

Pop-out

Existing house

Opening up existing space

Former Walls

Living

Entry hall

Kitchen-Dining

Converting a garage

Existing house

Former Garage

Close off doors—perhaps make windows

New carport

New slab

New sliding glass doors or windows

Adding a glazed sunroom

Glazed Sunroom

Existing house

Pushing out windows

Existing house

New dormers

New bay windows or greenhouse windows

Finishing an attic

Former attic

Office

Bath

Bedroom

Living

Stairway

Existing house

From sidewalk, Dutch colonial appears unchanged

Behind original house, new rooms stack up neatly on three levels

Adding on to this traditional Dutch colonial house required a clever juggling act. The owners needed lots of additional living space; at the same time, they wanted to preserve their home's old-fashioned charm. Their solution: A three-level addition to the back of the house that's wholly contemporary but that carries out the original house's theme in its horizontal clapboard siding and window details.

The addition encompasses 1,500 square feet of sunny, south-facing living space. At ground level, a new formal dining room opens onto a sizable deck for outdoor entertaining. Above this the owners cantilevered a master bedroom and bath suite, complete with its own deck. Three stories up is a television room. From the top deck, family and guests can enjoy a view of the city and distant mountains in elevated privacy.

Architect: Roderick Ashley.

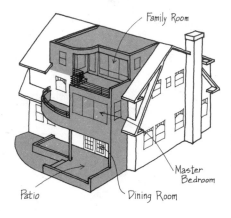

Traditional Dutch colonial gains square footage in back, retains its original look from the street.

Dining room's French doors open onto deck for informal alfresco meals.

Three-level addition *added 1,500 square feet—ground-floor dining room, second-floor master bedroom suite, third-floor TV room, and decks for outdoor living on all levels.*

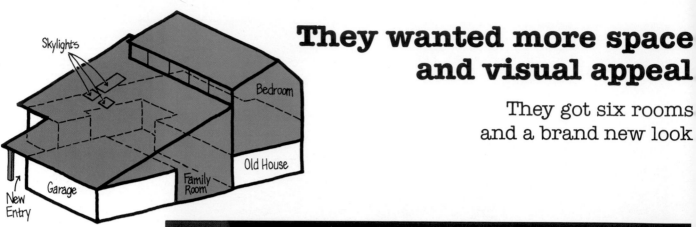

They wanted more space and visual appeal

They got six rooms and a brand new look

Skylights

Bedroom

Old House

Family Room

Garage

New Entry

Dotted lines show original house.

Above: *Once-flat house doubles in size, gains second story.* **Right:** *High ceiling, windows, doors open up kitchen to new family room.*

Originally this house was an ordinary-looking flat-roofed structure. The owners needed a great deal more space, and they wanted to improve the appearance of their home.

Their sloping-roofed addition nearly doubled the size of the house and transformed a plain exterior into a far more interesting one.

Inside are a new family room, three new bedrooms, and two new bathrooms. The new family room, built where a central atrium used to be, is now the heart of the house. It's a full two stories (18 feet) high. Bronzed glass in the room's large windows keeps down glare while preserving a light, open feeling.

All exterior walls were covered with stucco. The addition and the original house merge perfectly, presenting a far more attractive façade to the world than did the old house.

Architect: William Gratiot.

Above: Sloping roof, stucco exterior unite old and new. **Left:** New master bedroom overlooks backyard.

Front expansion gives old home a new face

Pushing out and up adds living room, bedroom, loft

A room addition on the front of a house has two advantages: it can dramatically alter the structure's street-side appearance, and it makes use of that often-expendable area, the front lawn.

The house on this page began as a weekend retreat. New owners wanted it for a permanent family residence, but they needed more functional space and wanted to update its appearance. For them, front lawn was unimportant, so the natural place to add and accomplish both their goals was in the front.

The house received a new shed-roof addition that reaches all the way to the municipality's height limit, giving views over neighboring houses to the ocean. The roof repeats the angle of the existing house's roof, helping to tie the structures together esthetically.

Downstairs is a new bedroom that opens onto a new, fenced-in patio. The room is windowless on three sides to insulate it from street noises.

Upstairs is the new living room with its views over the rooftops. To one side is a tea-for-two loft for even more dizzying views.

Architect: John Blanton.

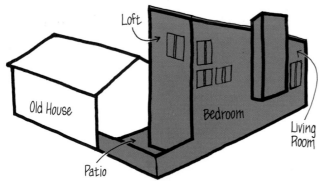

Dramatic addition gives front of plain house a brand-new look. There's drama inside, too, in sharp pitch of living-room ceiling and loft with spectacular view.

Two-story "lantern" brightens new study

New wing houses books, has sleeping space for guests, too

With a makeshift "office" jammed into a bedroom corner and a library of 2,000 books piled around the room, the owners of this house decided the time had come to create a proper study. Along with it, they wanted abundant daylight and space for overnight guests.

Their 275-square-foot addition meets all these requirements. The distinctive new study extends from one end of the original living room. An L-shaped, built-in desk and 200 running feet of bookshelves define the study area; two cushioned platforms nestled under the tower at the end of the room provide curl-up space for reading and spare beds for guests. The two-story, many-windowed tower acts as a giant "lantern," flooding the entire room with light.

Along with the tower, a sloping ceiling expands the space upward. The ceiling's height allows room above the bookcases for two clerestory windows that help balance the natural lighting.

The new wing parallels the pathway to the front door, creating an entry court that's accessible from the study through a set of French doors.

Architect: Donlyn Lyndon, Lyndon/Buchanan Associates.

Above right: Twenty-foot tower rises at one end of new combined study and guest room.
Right: In study, shelves hold nearly 2,000 books. Extended lower shelf creates knee-high counter.

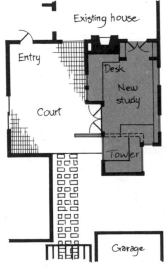

New wing off living room opens onto entry court. Tower is 8 feet square.

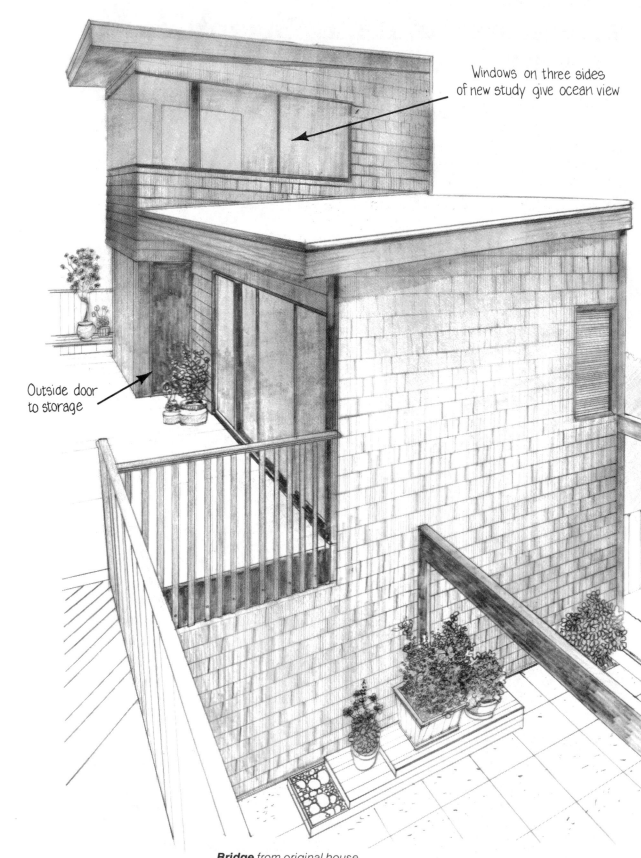

Windows on three sides of new study give ocean view

Outside door to storage

Bridge *from original house leads to new playroom / guest area and second-story study.*

No more room in the house, so they added on top of garage

Two-tiered expansion provides "crow's nest" study plus children's play area

Situated on a tiny lot, this house filled all available ground space. As their family grew, the owners needed more room for two active children and a study where the adults could enjoy quiet and privacy.

The only way to go was up, and the only place to go up was over the garage. The outcome was a two-room, two-level addition. The lower room accommodates guests when they are present, serving as a children's playroom at other times. Up a steep stairway is a "crow's nest" study, high enough to give a fine ocean view, and effectively separated from the play area.

Overlooking a back patio, a red tiled deck and bridge connect the new rooms with the main house. Exterior cedar shingles match the house siding.

Architect: John Blanton.

Stair ladder connects the playroom/guest room with hideaway study located above it.

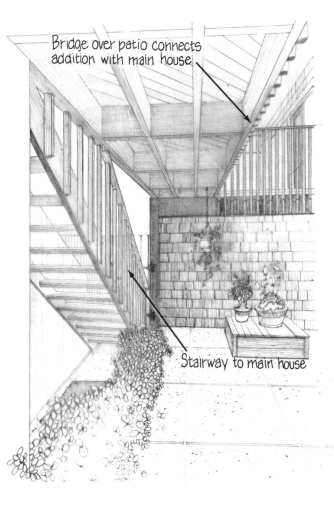

Bridge over patio connects addition with main house

Stairway to main house

Underneath *the new deck/bridge is a cement patio. Stairway at left leads up to main house.*

Stair ladder goes from playroom to "crow's nest" study

Narrow house gains light, space with two-story bay

Small expansion makes a big difference

A two-story-high pop-out with a peaked roof adds brightness and space to the interior of this narrow house. Mostly glass, the 8-foot-wide bay extends 3 feet from the house's southern end, flooding the interior with light.

The 19-foot-wide house, with an area of 1,445 square feet, has an unexpected sense of volume. Windows all along the second-floor living room's southern wall let the owners enjoy a broad city view; downstairs windows light up a bedroom. The cedar-paneled living room ceiling rises a lofty 17 feet above the floor; the bay's peak echoes the ceiling's shape and has the same paneling.

To create an illusion of width, low bands of narrow windows and strong horizontal muntins dividing the glass at waist level run across the full width of the house.

Designer: Kelly Crain, Crain-Cover Architects.

Triangular window and wood-ceilinged bay repeat lines and textures of tall living room.

Horizontal lines on exterior relieve severe vertical look of narrow, white-trimmed house.

Former "cracker box" house now has ample room

Expansion yields larger kitchen, entertainment area, open space

When the owners first purchased it, this 1930s house was poorly laid out, divided into many small rooms. None of the rooms took advantage of the spectacular westward view, overlooking a lake and a major city. The kitchen was dark and lacked an eating area; a long, narrow dining room obstructed traffic flow from the living room to the kitchen; and the upstairs bedrooms were dark and cramped. The owners needed more light and open space. In addition, they wanted the house to offer a multitude of environments, from an everyday kitchen to a gallery and sitting area.

Their addition redesigned interior spaces entirely and added onto the house's three levels. It pushed out the kitchen's west wall about 8 feet, extending a new bay window with an abundance of glass. This new bay became a breakfast area and focal point for the kitchen. Windows angled at 45° created an almost panoramic view, allowing the breakfaster to gaze both north and southwest.

The owners also wanted to free the dining room of its narrow, locked-in feeling. Again they pushed out, breaking up the exterior wall with a two-story window wall that reveals a breathtaking view. Not only does the new space allow for pleasant dining, but enough room is left over for an informal gallery/sitting area. This space creates a solarium for plants and insulates the quiet living room from the busy view.

Though the project added but little square footage upstairs, it eliminated what was the master bedroom suite's exterior wall. The bedroom was opened further by an interior balcony overlooking the tall dining room space and the two-story window wall.

Architect: Gary Sortun.

Above: Small but light and airy breakfast nook. **Below:** *Spectacular two-story window wall.*

Addition freed cramped kitchen, dining room spaces. Large windows face spectacular views.

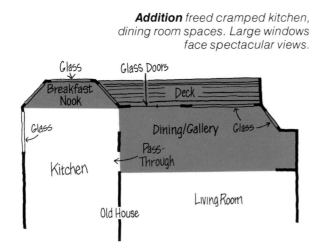

Present blends with past in ranch house addition

Doubling in size, weekend country home becomes more formal retreat

Comfort *exudes from new living room. Wood rafters add structural depth, counterpoint with flat wall surfaces.*

New deck off end of living room

Built-in *window seat offers a quiet reading area facing a stand of redwood trees.*

With an eye to making it a permanent residence someday, the owners of this century-old ranch house added on without sacrificing the traditional exterior appearance they liked so much.

Extending the gabled roof northward, the addition doubles the size of the original house. To change the interior's closed-in character, a large living room extends out into the redwood trees. This new room opens up the kitchen and dining areas; its windows and skylight bring them more light and a more spacious feeling. The whole addition then appears almost large enough to be considered "grand," but its simple clean lines and materials keep it from becoming cold and aloof. The exposed wood rafters are painted with a special paint that reflects light throughout the day so as to visually animate room space.

On a lower level, an extra bedroom, playroom, and storage area were added to accommodate weekend guests.

Finally, to take fullest advantage of the beautiful setting, a new deck was added on three sides of the house. It's shaded from direct afternoon sun by the nearby big trees. The end result is a blending of nature with architecture, and past with present, giving a wonderful simplicity.

Architect: William Turnbull, MLTW/Turnbull Associates.

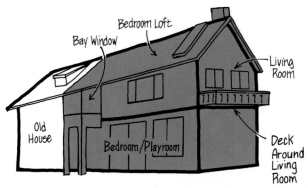

Sketch shows house doubled in size. **Top right:** New spacious feeling created by merging dining, living, and kitchen areas. **Right:** Kitchen pass-through brings cook into the conversation.

Past and present stand back-to-back

New two-story space presents an exciting departure in style

Bold new cube *is two stories tall and full of windows and light.*

The owners of this 1955 ranch house were happy with their home's original look and feel. But when the time came to add on more space, they were ready for something exciting and more contemporary. The result—this bold 1,080-square-foot addition—proves that past and present can stand back-to-back without detracting from each other.

From the street, the cube-shaped addition is little more than a horizontal sliver running along the roof peak to one side of the chimney. But face the addition straight on and you see a powerful two-story box where sunlight and views pour into west-facing double-glazed windows. Fifteen skylights bring in still more light and repeat the grid pattern established in the exterior windows. Numerous doors keep the room well ventilated on hot days.

Here everyone assembles for music, games, and talk. A loft above allows the artist in the family to work without feeling cut off from the activity. The formal living and dining rooms in the original house still get plenty of use.

Architects: Carolyn Widgery and Stuart Silk.

Above: Open floor plan features curved divider between conversation corner and game area. Artist's loft is overhead.
Right: Glass-paneled doors open to garden.

Seen from street, ranch house retains tailored, period look; addition barely looks over roof peak.

They needed a private bedroom and a room for music

They added an upstairs bedroom suite, converted a downstairs bedroom into a music room

New master bedroom and upper living room

Above: Tall, slanting windows of new second story face onto patio. *Below:* Upper level allows intimacy with wooded surroundings.

Stairway down to front entry

Before remodeling, this house had a master bedroom right off the front doorway; it didn't provide the privacy the owners wanted. Besides, one of the owners is a piano teacher who needed a room for lessons—a room situated so as not to disrupt life in the rest of the house.

Both problems were solved by the addition of a second-floor master bedroom suite, freeing the old master bedroom for lessons and practice.

The new second floor comprises a bedroom, bath, and large walk-in closets. The living room roof was also raised to match the height of the added second floor roof line, almost doubling the room's height and creating a very striking visual effect. Large slanted windows allow light to enter and afford fine views of the surrounding wooded hillsides.

An opening in the new bedroom's wall overlooks the living room, creating an interesting balconylike effect. The opening can be closed with cupboard-type doors.

Architect: Carl Day.

Balcony bridge *overlooks expanded living room. High bookshelves, plants, and art brighten upper walls. Deck also adjoins master bath.*

Stairway down to front entry

Bridge to bath, bedroom overlooks living room

Cottage reaches up for daylight

Tiny house gains light and space without losing charm

Opened-up kitchen wall *lets dining area share light from new kitchen windows; knee-braced opening keeps to cottage style.*

The cottage shown here sits on a pleasant two-acre coastal site. But until the remodel, the pleasantness stopped abruptly at the front door. Inside, the 1,500-square-foot house was dark and confining, its knot-holed redwood paneling having aged to a deep, almost black tone. Small aluminum-framed windows did little to relieve the darkness.

The new architect/owner and his wife, anxious to renovate the house without sacrificing its special character, saw the possibilities in the cottage and set about filling its cheerless interior with light and livability. A new 17-foot light tower on the southwestern side of the living room, the centerpiece of their remodel, enhances the character of the house while performing lighting and ventilating functions admirably.

The architect held down costs by staying on the former structure's foundation, yet made the house feel larger by raising the ceiling to the height of the original roof, pushing out the light-tower dormer, and removing a kitchen wall. Outdoors, adjacent to the front door, he created an angled deck that's bounded by lattice panels. A wisteria-covered frame defines the entry.

Architect: Obie Bowman.

Vented light tower *rises above roof plane of cottage like a stylized dormer; its window echoes lines of existing roof gables.*

Raised ceiling of living room exposes roof trusses. Under light-tower windows is couch with built-in bookshelves.

The open, roomy feeling of this townhouse belies its small size: only 960 square feet of floor space. The effect was achieved by an upward and outward expansion that involved several steps.

First, a cross-shaped upper level was added, providing sleeping space, a study alcove, and a bridge to an outside deck while leaving large openings for light to fall through upper windows and skylights to the main floor below.

The building code required either plywood interior shear walls or a steel frame to strengthen the added height. The frame was less expensive and far more desirable, enabling the owner to do away with cloistering interior walls altogether. The only enclosures are a bathroom and a child's room at the rear of the house.

The strengthening frames consist of two tall steel rectangles, inserted through the house levels at front and rear and ballasted by concrete under the garage floor. The frames also help support the new upper floor.

Finally, a 3-foot lateral extension—just enough for support posts to clear the existing outside stairway—made room for inside stairs to the new level, ample bedroom storage on that level, and a fireplace alcove underneath.

Architect: Daniel Solomon.

Above: High windows and skylights flood stairs with light. *Right:* Steel frame accents living room, dining room decor.

Small San Francisco house opens up and grows

Steel frame allows expansive interiors, new bedroom loft

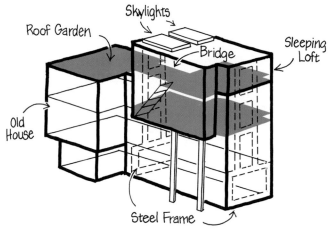

Roof Garden
Skylights
Bridge
Sleeping Loft
Old House
Steel Frame

Above: Steel frames and lateral extension make room for addition. **Left:** Loft bedroom faces bridge leading to roof garden.

Three-story house goes higher for views

A deft blend of old and new

The hillside location of this city house offered great view potential, but no owner had taken full advantage of it.

Remodeling the upper two levels captured breathtaking bay and city vistas and created a fourth-level family room loft with its own observation deck. Bedrooms were relocated to the second floor; rental units on the bottom level were left alone.

Changing the flat roof line to a gable peak made room for the bright new loft above the main living area on the third level. The loft, perching on columns in the center of the gabled volume, is rimmed on three sides by 3-foot-high walls. Glass doors open to the sunny deck at the rear of the house.

While the loft overlooks rooms below, those rooms look up past the half-walls to skylights in the high ceiling above. The openness gives both levels a greater sense of space and an interesting complexity in the way they're separate but related.

Design by Tanner & Van Dine Architects.

Below the gable, loft floats above main living level. Catwalk in foreground joins main stairwell.

Four-story remodel reaches up for views with new gabled roof line. Upper-level cantilevered bays add floor space.

Owners gain work/ entertainment room

Upstairs storage space becomes new loft

The architect who owns this house wanted new space for his expanding family. His design took advantage of a small attic and the attractive but inefficient cathedral ceiling in the living room.

Cutting through the roof, he fitted in a loft that extends over part of the living room. He used garage space and a closet to accommodate a stairway and landing behind an existing living room wall.

The new loft is a combination work, entertainment, and retreat space. It stays warm enough on many winter evenings that the owners can turn off the heat downstairs and read or watch television in their new perch. In summer months, the three new clerestory windows let out heat, increase air circulation, and flood the once-dark living room with light.

Architect: Russell Barto.

Labels: Roof Removed, Windows, Rail, Loft, Old House, Living Room, Garage, Stairs

Loft was fitted into house with minimal exterior change. Inside, loft is small but well designed. Large windows improve air circulation.

Rail overlooks living room

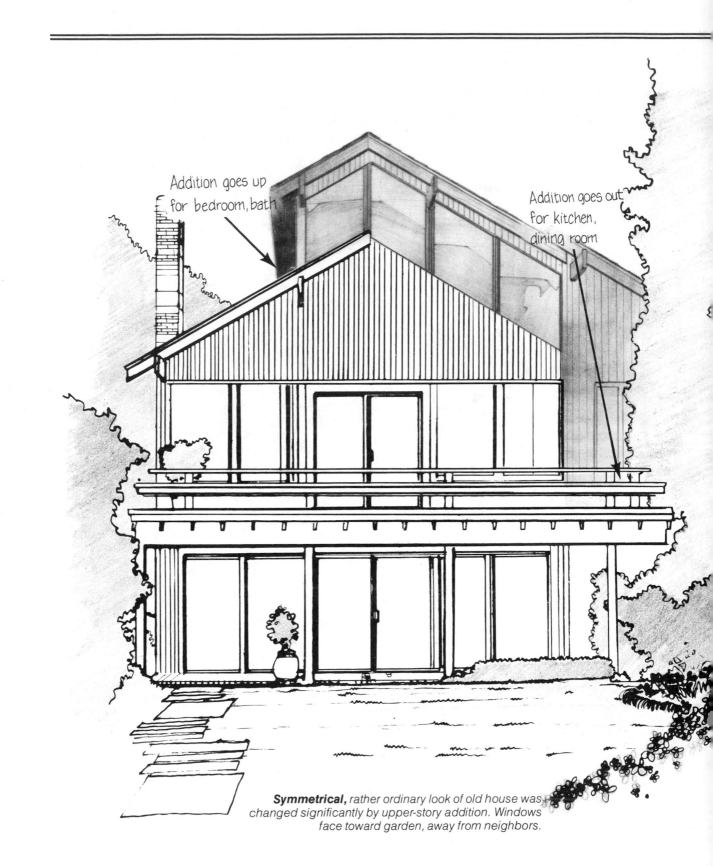

Addition goes up for bedroom, bath

Addition goes out for kitchen, dining room

Symmetrical, rather ordinary look of old house was changed significantly by upper-story addition. Windows face toward garden, away from neighbors.

Lakefront cottage grows up and out

Without crowding lot, owners gain new kitchen, dining room, master bedroom

This small home on a long, narrow lakefront lot presented its owners with a number of challenges. They needed more house, and they wanted landscaping that would give privacy and at the same time make their small garden as large as possible.

The final plans called for pushing up through the roof to add a master bedroom and bath, and pushing out toward one side fence to accommodate a new kitchen and dining room. The old kitchen became a study.

With window expanses only on the garden side, and with a sweeping shed roof, the house has privacy from neighbors and excellent views channeled down the long lot toward the lake.

A street-side fence and plantings along the property's perimeter also help ensure privacy. The garden, mostly of evergreen shrubs but including deciduous trees to let in winter sunlight, creates the illusion of a much larger area.

Architect: Reid Morgan.

Jalousie windows bring fresh air into kitchen

Ceiling panel lines give visual spaciousness to bedroom

Above: New kitchen has exposed-beam ceiling with skylight. **Left:** Odd-shaped windows in roomy bedroom have special slat blinds.

They decided the only way to go was up

Result: Light-flooded artist's studio

The owners of this house, situated on a confining canyonside lot, wanted a versatile workspace that a future owner could convert to guest quarters or a family room. With no space to add on at ground level, the architect located the new studio over the old garage, which sits at the lowest point of the property (the house and garden step uphill behind).

To flood the studio with natural light, the architect ran an arched skylight along the ridge line. Supporting it are 2 by 8 rafters which cross in scissor fashion; lower down, horizontal 2 by 6s cross-brace the roof structure.

At the rear of the studio, two sets of double doors open to the garden. Between them is a full bathroom; its ceiling is at normal height, its top floored with pine for a potential sleeping loft.

The exterior has been clad in cedar siding; red window trim adds a bright touch. The roof is fire-retardant corrugated aluminum.

Architect: Michael Rachlin.

Skylit ridge of studio grabs natural illumination. Three-part window in room's west-facing front echoes exterior roof line; center section swings open for ventilation.

Cedar siding integrates new studio and old garage; high above, curved sheet acrylic skylight unit, custom-made in 4-foot sections, crowns addition.

They wanted a second story and their own space

Above all, the new master bedroom is private

Originally the owners of this house converted the garage into a master bedroom, connecting it to the main house with a lanailike covered patio. After a while they began to wish for more privacy than their ground-floor addition offered them, so they decided on a second-story addition.

Like the earlier addition, the new second story blends in nicely with the original structure. It includes a master bedroom, an adjoining bathroom, a vanity with a double sink, and a large walk-in closet. Also added was a small deck overlooking the backyard, reached through sliding glass doors from either the bedroom or the bath.

Downstairs, the addition of a fireplace to the old master bedroom converted it into a family room. The floor of the enclosed patio was built up to the level of the adjoining living room and retiled. The existing patio wall was pushed out slightly, and sliding glass doors were added to open to the outdoor patio and garden. These modifications let in light and allowed the new space between the dining room and family room to become not only a circulation area for the new stairway to the second floor, but also a small gallery and music area. The glass wall and doors on the first floor reiterate those of the upstairs bedroom suite, thereby integrating the second-story addition with the main house.

Architects: Churchill-Zlatunich-Lorimer.

Both new master bedroom and bathroom open onto deck. Bathroom has large storage area.

Viewed from front, second-floor addition appears small, simple, unobtrusive.

CUTTING COSTS:
Tips for remodeling economically

Saving money is a subject dear to the hearts and wallets of all homeowners, especially when it's time to remodel or add on. Many remodeling projects—particularly room additions—are expensive undertakings, so it pays to consider a spectrum of cost-cutting ideas.

Two cautions on cutting costs

First, unless you're careful, cutting costs can mean cutting quality. Don't settle for what's cheaper if it means that the finished product will suffer. And don't try to do work yourself unless you feel comfortable with the job at hand and confident of your skills.

Second, remember that usually what you save in money you spend in time. You have to be willing to devote weekend hours looking for building materials or your spare time cleaning up, installing insulation, or putting up gypsum board.

Money-saving tips

Below we've listed a number of homeowner-tested ways to save money when remodeling:

• **Do all the work yourself.** If you have time—and if you're confident that your skills as a designer and builder will create a new space that will be an asset to your property—you can do the whole job yourself, from start to finish. Although you'll spend a lot of time, you'll spend fewer dollars, and you could gain a large measure of satisfaction.

• **Act as your own contractor.** Here again, you'll need to spend a lot of time in order to save yourself money. And to be your own contractor, you must have sufficient building knowledge to orchestrate the numerous jobs that must be done, plus enough managerial skill to supervise and schedule the subcontractors needed for those jobs. You'll work hard, but you'll also have an opportunity to control quality at close range.

• **Hire less expensive labor.** If you're going to act as your own contractor, you will be able to hire experienced students or retired or moonlighting craftspeople and construction workers. These people will most likely charge less than the workers hired by a professional general contractor.

• **Prepare the site yourself.** Before construction begins, you can do any necessary demolition, such as tearing up concrete and pulling down walls.

• **Do all the cleanup.** Normally, a contractor will see to it that the building site is cleaned up each day and will charge you for the necessary labor. You can agree with the contractor to do daily cleanup and to do all necessary cleanup and hauling after the job is completed.

• **Install the insulation.** One of the most common jobs that home-owners do during the construction process is installing insulation. It's a relatively simple project, and doing it yourself can save some labor costs.

• **Do some finishing work.** Many homeowners have saved money by doing sanding, sealing, and painting themselves. Also, you can install such hardware as cabinet pulls and light fixtures. Another cost-cutting measure is to apply wallpaper or other wall coverings yourself.

• **Check wholesale and retail suppliers for seconds and sales on fixtures and appliances.** A second is often as good as the unflawed product, and flaws are usually insignificant. Just make sure such items are in good working order.

• **Buy directly from the manufacturer.** Manufacturers of such materials as tile, skylights, and flooring often sell to the public at prices lower than retail.

• **Use recycled house parts.** If you're willing to immerse yourself completely in your remodeling project, you can haunt wrecking and salvage yards (look in the Yellow Pages under "Wrecking Contractors") for treasures removed from demolished buildings. If you're after something specific, ask various wreckers to keep an eye out for it. Also, watch for demolitions in progress. You can often learn in advance about the demolition of a building by reading the legal notices in a local building trade paper.

Even a small addition can make a big difference

Pushing out a wall creates a roomy breakfast nook

The kitchen of this house was a little too dark for its owners. Besides more light, they also wanted a breakfast area and a new deck, but they didn't want to reduce the size of their backyard.

The overhang of the kitchen's shedlike roof presented an excellent opportunity for expansion without major structural changes. The addition pushed out a kitchen wall to the limit of the roof overhang. Built inward from the new wall, an 8-foot window seat obviates the need for a full set of chairs around the table and provides a spacious feeling in very little actual available space. Vertical tongue-and-groove hemlock paneling was used for the interior.

A door and large picture window open onto a new deck, added over what was once a small concrete patio so that no backyard space was sacrificed.

Architect: Ted Granger.

Kitchen wall has pass-through to breakfast area

Window seat eliminates need for space-consuming chairs in small dining area. New nook looks into backyard. Light-colored hemlock wall paneling helps keep room bright.

Door opens to new deck

New family room off kitchen creates intimate relationship with outdoors

Modern sky windows blend with 1906 house

Sky windows *of addition continue sloping roof line of original house. Behind balcony, a small deck.*

Doors of addition open onto garden

The owners of this hilltop house wanted a family room with an easy, natural relationship to the outdoors and a better view of the ocean in the distance.

The lines of the 1906 house weren't marred in the slightest by the addition of a sun-filled family room at the rear. Done at the same time as a kitchen remodel, the new room blends well with the rest of the house without trying to conceal the fact that it's an addition.

The room was designed with a sloping sky window, pitched at the same angle as the roof, so the lines of the addition flow into those of the house. A small deck added behind the sky window opens an upstairs bedroom to the outdoors (a door was fitted into an old window opening).

The north-facing room is a great place for plants. Large containers rest on the brick floor; hanging ones are suspended on pulleys. Because it's a few steps down from the kitchen, the room has the benefit of an 11-foot-high ceiling. The sky window rises for 15 feet at the top.

Architect: Val Thomas.

Brick-floored room is showcase for hanging plants, art works. Floodlights recessed in ceiling enhance natural lighting.

See-over kitchen half-wall

A natural extension of the older structure

New library/guest room harmonizes with rest of house

The owners of this house wanted a library, but they also needed a room for overnight guests. The addition they built is such a natural extension of the older structure that it doesn't appear to be an addition at all.

The owners designed the addition themselves, with the help and advice of the builder. The new library/guest room extends a bay window out into the backyard—a bay that matches one on the opposite side of the house. Inside are built-in bookcases and a window seat. At both ends of the room, built-in seats convert to single beds.

To match the line of the old house with the added room, the walls of the master bedroom and an adjoining bedroom were pushed out. The new space off the master bedroom became a small study.

Before the new addition, the back patio could be reached only through a child's bedroom. Along with the new room, the owners added a new hallway and a new rear entry for easier access to the backyard.

During construction, as many materials as possible were saved from the removed portions of exterior wall and roof; these were used on the new exterior. Recycled doors and windows became part of the addition, too.

Builder: David French.

Old House

Library/Guest Room

Bay window in new room matches one on other side of house. Inside, built-in seat is also bed with storage underneath.

1920s bungalow opens up inside and out

Dark little house opens to garden outdoors, daylight indoors

When the present owners first saw it, the best things about this small bungalow were its price (affordable) and its location (close to downtown). The rest wasn't so good: it was dark and deteriorated, and had an inconvenient floor plan. But they liked the house's character and felt its deep lot had potential for expansion.

The plan that developed was a combination remodel and addition. The floor plan of the front of the house underwent only a few modifications—reorienting the front porch, blocking off some interior doors, and moving the door to the kitchen.

The back of the house changed more dramatically. The new kitchen occupies the space of the old one, plus some of the old back bedroom and utility porch. A new master bedroom and breakfast nook were added; skylights and raised ceilings in the new rooms create volume and brightness.

Sliding glass doors from the bedroom and kitchen now open onto a deck and garden beyond. On warm summer evenings, the deck, with its built-in hot tub, is a favorite area for informal entertaining.

Architect: Steven Goldstein, Environment Plus.

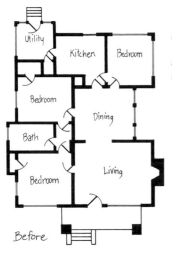

House grew from 1,165 to 1,465 square feet. Colored area shows part of house that has been changed.

Angled addition at back of house leads to entertainment deck, accessible from both kitchen and new bedroom.

Previously the kitchen of this house was too cramped for the owners. And it didn't take advantage of the view of a nearby valley and adjacent large trees. In addition to a roomier kitchen and an enhanced view, the owners wanted a space for family acitivities, reading, games, conversation, and study.

The addition shown here maintained the flavor of the existing structure. The kitchen grew out, continuing the slope of the existing roof and the beamed ceiling of the existing kitchen. Custom-made floor tiles matched the new floor with the old. The walls of the newly enlarged room are finished in resawn redwood siding and painted white. Large windows provide an excellent north view where none existed before. The slope of the ceiling gives a sense of height and opens the room to the trees that branch out above. New closet space is handy, and a fireplace enhances the new gathering area with a warm intimacy.

Outside the kitchen, a new deck creates an outdoor living and entertainment area. A solid railing on one side provides privacy from neighboring homes, while an open railing faces the valley and vista.

Architects: Churchill-Zlatunich-Lorimer AIA.

Kitchen extension adds dining space, gives view of valley

New deck provides outdoor entertainment area

Kitchen grew out around a tree. Windows welcome the outdoors in. Tiles in new dining area match those in old kitchen.

"Sun" bridge leads to new bedroom wing

House gains master bedroom suite, views, and solar heating

To take advantage of views to a canyon beyond, a new master bedroom suite was situated on a small ridge behind this house. Linking the addition with the main part of the house in front is a covered bridge, which not only creates a dramatic passageway but also serves as a solar collector, providing auxiliary heat for both the master bedroom and the main house.

Running east to west and spanning a gully behind the house, the bridge has three large double-glazed sliding doors facing south. Low winter sun warms the tiled concrete slab floor; a fan and duct system helps circulate heat from the bridge throughout the house. In summer, overhangs block the high summer sun and reduce heat buildup. On very hot days, glass doors at each end close off the bridge; the sliding doors can be opened to let heat escape.

The designer carried the lines of the bridge's gable roof out over the old house and to a living room addition in front, raising the roof line in the existing living room. All the roofs are clad with corrugated steel, giving the house a uniform look.

Designer: Wayne Leong.

Solar bridge links main house at left with bedroom suite at right; concrete columns under bridge help support it. Three sliding glass doors facing almost due south bring in winter sun; overhang keeps out high summer sun.

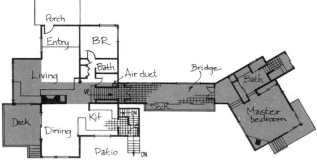

Tiled hallway on bridge collects and stores heat; glass doors at each end of bridge can be used to control heat distribution to rest of house.

1920s home gains space, light, and a lean-to kitchen

Old kitchen becomes family dining room

The lean-to was surely one of man's earliest constructed shelters. That old basic form appears again in this new kitchen. Simple to construct, it allows a great deal of open interior space.

The main framework of the trusses that support the sloping roof is built of 2 by 6s; smaller members are 2 by 4s bolted between them. And between the 2 by 6s is a space just wide enough for recessed track lighting.

The old kitchen in this 1920s home was dark and cramped. The new kitchen has large vertical windows in the back wall and translucent glass panes in the roof to provide plenty of northern light and to give a pleasant garden view. There's plenty of space for table and chairs, as well as more than enough cabinets and maple butcher-block counter tops.

Architect: Tom Devine.

Exposed roof trusses give room a feeling of spaciousness. Lean-to has clean, simple lines.

Translucent glass panes soften direct sun

Clear glass gives garden view

POP-OUTS: Making every inch count

Pushing out a wall to create a narrow pop-out can yield that crucial little bit of space that can transform a dark, cramped room into a spacious, light-filled one. A pop-out that's only 1 to 3 feet deep can accommodate additional storage cabinets in your kitchen or dining room, an extra closet in your bedroom, or even a tub or shower in a bathroom.

In the process of gaining space, you can also gain light. A glazed pop-out can flood an entire room with cheery sunshine and admit a previously cut-off view. If privacy is a consideration, you can let in light through a skylight roof on the pop-out, through small windows in the pop-out's side walls, or through a window in the wall above the pop-out. A tried-and-true version of the pop-out—the bay window—also lets in plenty of light.

Pop-outs that are cantilevered outward require new floor joists attached to the house's existing joists. Other pop-outs will require a small foundation for support. You can extend the existing roof line or create a new roof for the pop-out.

Glazed foot-wide pop-out floods kitchen with light, adds 21 feet of storage and counter space. Architect: Stewart Ankrom of Griggs, Lee, Ruff, Ankrom/Architects.

Cantilevered pop-out, 2 feet deep, creates new bedroom closets. Window above lets in plenty of light. Architect: Jerry Smania.

Pop-out on its own foundation makes room for built-in buffet in dining room; windows in side walls admit light. Designer: Norman Ridenour.

Glass eaves brighten new kitchen-family room

Shed-roofed addition gains extra space and light

Glass eaves lend a gallerylike quality to this kitchen-family room addition, bringing natural light and treetop views into the house.

The architect-owner continued the roof line at the back of his two-story house, creating a shed addition. Then, to gain light and even more space, he extended it with an L-shaped periphery covered in glass.

Large beams that rest on painted Tuscan columns carry the load of the solid roof extension. Glass eaves continue down one side and wrap around a corner of the addition, daylighting the nar-

row kitchen and brightening the rest of the 16 by 26-foot space. Under the eaves at one end, windows extend to the wainscoting near a dining table and fireplace enclosure; on the side, the glass stops above the kitchen cabinets.

A kitchen peninsula that steps down to become a ledge behind an L-shaped sofa ties the two rooms together. At the same time, a change of level helps separate the space: one step leads from the kitchen up to the family room. Heating ducts and wiring run beneath the raised floor.

Architect: Don Bowman, Mithun Bowman Emrich.

Shed-roofed addition *ends with glass-topped extension; glass continues around one side, brightening kitchen. Chimney juts through solid panel in bank of glass.*

See-through roof *over kitchen cabinets lights counters and small office area at end. Track lighting hides behind beam.*

Large space *is divided by kitchen peninsula, which drops down to become ledge around family room sofa. Lights above counter hang from sloping ceiling.*

Addition echoes charm of original house

New porch enhances old farmhouse's atmosphere of repose

Country kitchen *was updated, but flavor of old house was preserved, including original fieldstone fireplace.*

A happy marriage of old and new—that's the phrase that best describes the addition to this 1860s farmhouse, also pictured on our cover.

Over the years, the farmhouse had seen many additions and changes. This latest remodel added two bedrooms, expanded the master bath, and created an attractive porch above a new garage.

Separated from the updated country kitchen by French doors and a small enclosed bridge, the spacious porch is used for dining, parties, or simply lounging. In winter, the tile floor collects solar heat through skylights and wraparound windows. At times, enough heat is stored to help warm the rest of the house.

In summer, screens replace all the glass panels, and the skylights are shaded. Prevailing breezes make the porch an ideal summer retreat.

Architect: Lyndon/Buchanan Associates.

Porch addition *(at right) handsomely complements original farmhouse. Porch extends living area to take advantage of small creek below.*

Inside porch pavilion, *bright and airy surroundings invite casual pursuits. In summer, breezes wafting through screens provide cool comfort; in winter, solar heat streaming in through skylights and windows is collected in tile floor.*

Understated and almost symmetrical, *1907 farmhouse has found new vitality in a remodel that played up assets, improved floor plan.*

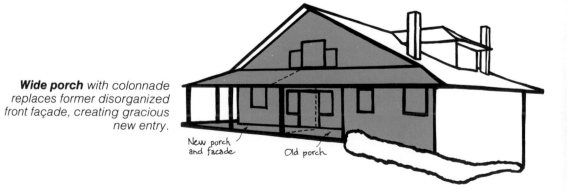

Wide porch with colonnade replaces former disorganized front façade, creating gracious new entry.

New porch and facade

Old porch

Architectural magic opens up 1907 farmhouse

Adding space without adding on

For this remodel, the architects retained the charm of this shingled farmhouse while improving the layout. The owners, a young family of four, didn't need any more space than the big house offered, but they did need help with the hodgepodge of rooms, a result of earlier remodels.

To produce a formal character, the interior plan was rearranged; now, a bright central gallery extends from the repositioned entry to French doors at the opposite side of the house. The gallery divides the house, with family room and master suite on one side and living room, dining room, and kitchen on the other. Outside, wide stairs lead to the back garden and a lake beyond.

To open up the interior further, one of the four upstairs bedrooms was sacrificed. Removing part of the bedroom's floor made way for a two-story entry hall with a grand staircase wrapping around one wall and over the front door. The remaining bedroom space serves as a game room.

Windows and doors were replaced and relocated; a new colonnade and porch make the front façade more symmetrical and dignified.

Architects: Cardwell/Thomas Associates.

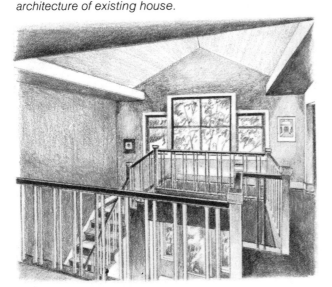

Opening the house vertically created dramatic, bright entry stairwell that complements architecture of existing house.

Central gallery extends from front to back, bringing in light and opening up space.

INTERIOR CHANGES: Gaining space without adding on

What can you do if your house feels cramped and inefficient, but it just isn't possible to expand its perimeters any further? If you can't add on, consider redefining and opening up the space that already exists.

Simply taking down walls or raising the ceiling can produce a feeling of surprising spaciousness. Be as bold or as restrained as you wish—remove a single wall to join two rooms together or open up your entire house to make one large great-room. You can remove a whole ceiling, leaving rafters and sheathing exposed, or push up just one portion of it.

Taking down walls

Knocking down one or more interior walls can transform a cluster of boxy, cramped rooms into a single large, bright space. For example, removing a wall between an isolated, too-small kitchen and an adjacent family room can create a roomy area for family and social activity that allows the cook to participate, too.

You can use a number of devices to define rooms within an opened-up space. Changes in level—different floor levels, connected by steps, or different ceiling heights—help to separate living areas and can add drama

as well. Another technique is to use low dividers, such as half-walls, counters, or islands, to mark off rooms, yet maintain openness. Even different floor coverings can define and separate "rooms" within a large, open area.

Before you knock down any wall, though, it's crucial to know whether it's a bearing wall—one that carries part of the weight of the floor above—or a nonbearing one. If you want to remove a bearing wall, you'll need to support the load by other means. Before you decide to remove any wall, be sure you know what wires or pipes are concealed in

With wall gone, *kitchen and family room are now one bright, open space. Two posts mark where wall was removed; island and tile floor suggest kitchen boundaries. Architect: Gerald Lee.*

Dramatic rectangular opening *surrounds recessed skylight well with two shafts; oversize joists around opening pick up load from interrupted ceiling joists. Architect: Victor H. Lee.*

that wall and have a plan for re-routing them.

Raising the ceiling

Often, there's an overlooked area right above you with good potential for opening up space—your attic. Removing the ceiling and reclaiming some or all of the attic volume can make a room seem bigger and brighter without altering the basic roof shape. The options are many, from simply removing the gypsum board ceiling to expose the existing joists, rafters, and sheathing to complex, engineered projects that carefully redistribute roof loads.

Unless you plan to remove only the gypsum board, making changes that affect the geometry and structural integrity of a roof will require the advice of an architect or structural engineer. In a typical gable-roofed house, the sloping rafters and horizontal ceiling joists form a rigid isosceles triangle, propped up at both ends of its base by bearing walls. The walls carry the vertical load of the roof to the foundation; the weight from the roof pushes down and out on the walls. The joists lock everything together and keep the walls vertical.

If you remove joists, the roof structure will be weakened un-less you do something to maintain the integrity of the triangle or redistribute the roof's load. Solutions include removing some joists and doubling up others, tying the roof rafters together with collar ties, or taking some of the roof load off the walls and carrying it with beams added at the ridge or along the rafters.

Raising the ceiling also involves a few trade-offs. The increased volume will require more energy for heating and cooling. In addition, ceilings can mask pipes, wires, and ducts, all of which must be rerouted, as well as insulation, which must be added in some other manner.

Tall, angled end wall rises to raised ceiling. *Room-long beam was added to support the rafters; posts in end walls carry beam's load to foundation. Architect: Tom Lukes, Holewinski and Blevens.*

Single soaring volume is organized around two *central posts that carry roof load. Rafters and sheathing are left exposed. Architect: James W. Christopher, Brixen & Christopher.*

Atrium opens up, reorganizes living space

They took down interior walls, didn't add a foot

This ranch-style house had enough floor space, but it was poorly organized. The family room was cut off, and you had to walk through the dining room to get to the living room. The owners knew there must be a better answer—and they also wanted a separate dining room.

The new design solved all the problems in a single stroke. The architect removed some interior walls and created a central atrium with all the living spaces radiating off it; the atrium serves both as the front entry and as the focal point of the house. By cutting corners off the living room and family room and walling in almost half the kitchen to make a home-plate-shaped dining room, she corrected the house's shortcomings without adding a single square foot.

Architect: Pamela Seifert.

From front door, *you see ridge-wrapping skylight over tiled atrium. Living room is at left of casual sitting area, kitchen at right.*

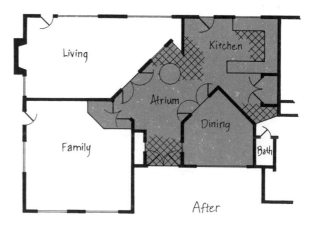

570-square-foot cottage doesn't grow an inch

Inside is an ellipse cut out for sleeping, seating

When the owners—an architect and a designer—set about remodeling their tiny cottage, they immediately began looking for a way to make the interior seem less cramped. They decided on a single bold shape—the ellipse—to define the living area, then placed dining room, kitchen, bathroom, and bedroom around it. The ellipse is actually a curving partition of gypsum board over stud framing, with cutouts for built-in seating and openings to the bedroom and dining room.

Fitting behind and partly exposed to the living room is the compact bedroom. Its rear wall contains floor-to-ceiling bookshelves with another unexpected detail: a concealed door in the bookcase wall leads to the bathroom. Built into the wall opposite the books (the back of the curved partition) are a bed, a desk, and drawers for linens.

A tightly organized kitchen opens directly to the dining area, which in turn opens to the living room.

The windows and doors, salvaged from other bungalows, enhance its cottagelike quality.

Architect: Buzz Yudell.

Curved partition *has cutouts for seating. Deepest cutout (far left) is bedroom; cushion at foot of bed supplements seating in living room.*

Ellipse dominating living spaces continues outside in curved steps. Bookcase wall echoes curve.

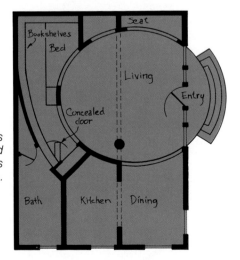

Tiny bungalow
gets lofty ceiling

Twin beams and slender pillar support rafters at midspan

The main living area of this little bungalow gained a new feeling of spaciousness and a clean, contemporary look without the addition of a single square foot of floor space. What did the trick was raising the ceiling.

To strengthen and support the roof after removal of the supporting joists, two wooden beams now run between the end walls, supporting the rafters at midspan. The architect wanted to keep the beam size small, so he added a columnar wall section for extra support near the painted prefab fireplace. The red pipes are collar ties; they connect the beams to create a strong, rigid triangular roof structure.

Architect: Doug Lowe, Solberg + Lowe.

Bright and airy, the main living area of this house gains a feeling of space from lofty, updated ceiling.

Little bungalow's gable roof allowed plenty of room for upward expansion.

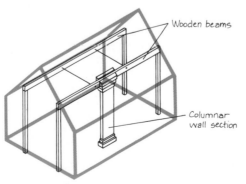

Wooden beams

Columnar wall section

Raising the ceiling transforms dark Victorian

Walls come down, ceiling goes up

A Queen Anne-style Victorian, this house had dark, cramped little rooms when the present owner bought it, intending to renovate it eventually. When the time came to remodel the living space on the top floor, he and his architect decided to open up the entire space by tearing out walls and removing the ceiling. The architect chose to leave the joists, rafters, and skip sheathing exposed. To bring in more light, he added a 15-foot-long skylight near the roof ridge and a lower, openable one near the small kitchen.

To comply with local building codes, which specified R-19 insulation, most of the old roof was removed, rigid foam insulation was mounted on the exterior, and new sheathing and shingles were added.

Inside the house, half-walls and counters help divide the open floor space into living and dining areas, kitchen, and bedrooms.

Architect: Dan Phipps.

Joists, rafters, and sheathing are exposed in Victorian remodel; range hood in open kitchen hangs from joists.

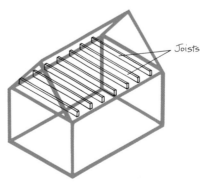

Open floor plan *adds feeling of spaciousness; half-walls and counters help divide space.*

Old house is strikingly modernized by addition

Dining and lounging area flood the house with light

Before remodeling, this was a dated, dark house on a beautiful piece of lakeside land. Besides needing more space for entertaining, the owners wanted to open the house to light and to a view of the lake.

The project restructured existing interior spaces and added on a greenhouse-section dining room that helps flood the house with light and gives superb views of the lake and surrounding countryside.

The actual added space is less than 200 square feet. The old living room wall was done away with, and a new 8-foot extension was enclosed with a glass wall and slanted glass sky windows. The new space is for dining or lounging and for enjoying views of the lake and a terraced garden.

The house's existing interior was redesigned so all living areas open up and focus, through the addition, on the spectacular view of the lake.

Architects: Boutwell, Gordon, Beard and Grimes.

Small, simple addition wrought startling changes. Glass-paneled wall gives great view of lake.

Slanted sky windo and glass walls give lake view

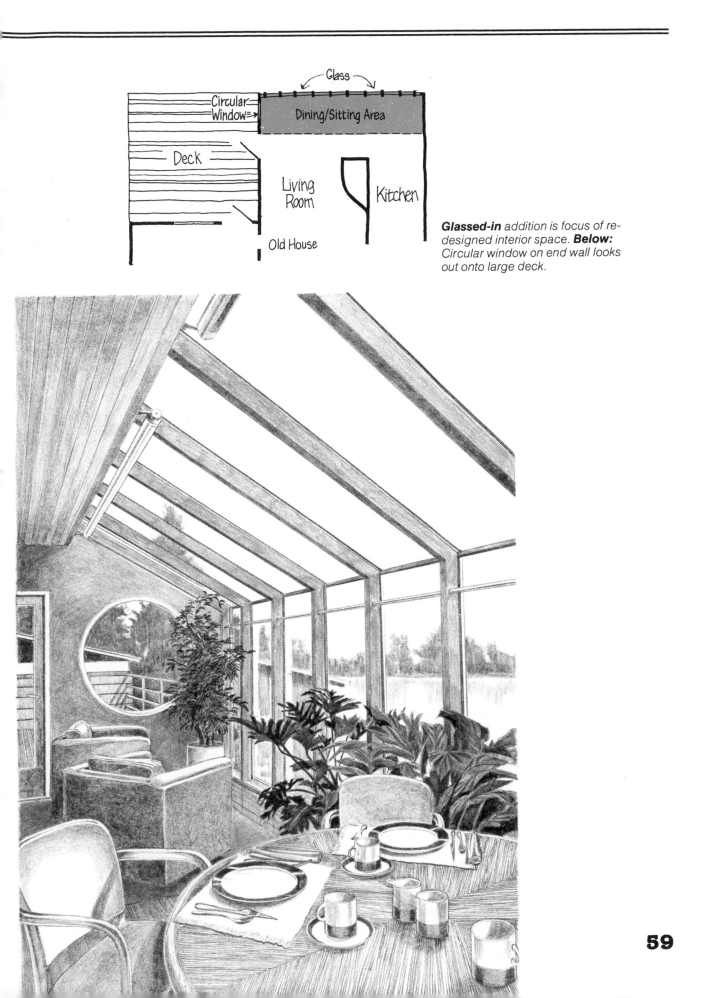

Glass

Circular
Window⇒

Dining/Sitting Area

Deck

Living
Room

Kitchen

Old House

Glassed-in addition is focus of redesigned interior space. **Below:**
Circular window on end wall looks
out onto large deck.

BRINGING THE OUTDOORS IN:
Sunrooms and greenhouse rooms

In almost any setting, a glazed sunroom or greenhouse room has lots of appeal. It's a beautiful, relatively simple way to bring light into your home and create a feeling of openness. And a glazed room can often provide an energy bonus in the form of passive solar heating.

For a sunroom, you'll need to use conventional framing, with plenty of windows and skylights. A greenhouse room, usually all glass, can be custom-built or constructed from a kit.

Bringing in light

Many older homes, and even some newer ones, have dark little rooms, and dimly lighted hallways. Often, a glazed addition can help relieve a somber interior, opening a home to new views and bringing the outdoors inside. And, of course, it can be an ideal place for plants.

Because glazed rooms make the most of even minimal amounts of light, they're an especially good add-on idea for brightening a room in geographical areas with many overcast days.

Tapping the sun's energy

Passive solar heating—a simple method of heating a room directly with the sun's radiation—comes naturally to a glazed addition. To make the most of the sun's warmth, your sunroom or greenhouse room should face due south (the direction of greatest solar exposure), unless you live in an area where summer

Battery of skylights and large double-glazed windows put sun to work in new sunroom. Architect: Stephen Lasar.

Glazed wall sections create dining room between kitchen and storage area. Architect: Clement Chen.

heat is more of a problem than winter cold. Then you may want to orient your room to the north or east to block out some of the sun.

The greater the window area in the south wall, the more heat the room will receive. To trap and hold in the heat, use double or triple-glazed windows; they have two or three layers of glass with dead air space between layers. A tile or masonry floor will help absorb and radiate heat. On chilly nights, use window coverings.

Troubleshooting your addition

You should be aware of some potential pitfalls in glazed additions. Unless properly constructed, they can be plagued by drafts or leaks. To prevent this, it's important to apply weatherstripping to windows and doors and seal with caulking and flashing where the new structure meets the original house. At the same time, though, proper ventilation is necessary to prevent condensation and eliminate excess heat buildup.

Direct sunlight may discolor upholstery, fade rugs, and dry out wood floors. It can also cause excessive heat buildup. To control the sun's effects, install roll-up shades of bamboo, fabric, vinyl, or aluminum, inside or outside. Reflective film on the windows can reduce glare by up to 80 percent. Outdoors, strategically placed overheads, trellises, and trees can block and filter excess sunlight.

Curved greenhouse addition captures sun's warmth on overcast days. Architect: Stuart Goforth.

Studio-greenhouse addition sits above entryway with view of trees.

Two-story sunroom captures solar heat

Big results from 7-foot extension

A narrow extension gives a big solar boost to this 1930s house. Because of setback requirements, the owners could extend the house only 7 feet. But that still provided enough surface area for glass in the roof and walls to make an effective solar room.

With its southeast exposure, the room gets ample sunlight from morning through midday, but little of the hotter, late-afternoon rays.

The existing first-floor office and kitchen and second-floor master bedroom open onto the addition. For privacy and heat control, three sets of doors can close off the bedroom. Mini-blinds covering all the new glassed areas also provide privacy and reflect sunlight away.

Two-way paddle fans help move warm air around the house. In cooler months, the fans drive heat downward so it can enter adjacent rooms. In hotter months, the fans can be reversed to pull heat from the interior and draw it upward to a 25-foot-high thermal chimney, where it exits through openable louvers.

Outside, the addition's roof pitch and height and its clapboard siding match the existing structure. Long panels of tempered glass rest on the exposed rafters. Inside, hexagonal pavers extend throughout the addition and into the kitchen.

Architects: Holland, East & Duvivier.

Second-floor balcony projects from master bedroom over new family room. Two-way fans move heated air into living spaces or up thermal chimney. Clapboard wall is old exterior.

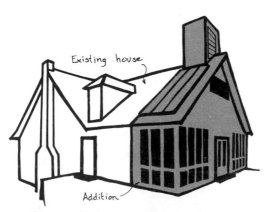

Glass-walled room with thermal chimney opens to new wraparound deck.

New sunroom blends seamlessly with existing home

Many-windowed room is energy-efficient, too

Meticulous design and painstaking workmanship resulted in a sunroom so well integrated that it's virtually impossible to tell from the outside where the original house ends and the addition begins.

On sunny winter days, the sunroom not only heats itself but also helps to heat the rest of the house. Overhead glazing and small-paned casement windows admit sunlight; warm air flows through a door at the rear of the addition into rooms on the home's east side. A fan-and-duct system can be used to assist the natural distribution of heat, when desired.

At night, the room requires no heat from the home's conventional furnace; the warmth stored in the concrete floor—and an efficient wood-burning stove—keep the space comfortable, even on the coldest nights.

Architect: Gerry Ives, Lamb & Ives.

Small-paned casement windows *admit more than woodland vista; they're efficient solar "collectors" in winter and can be opened for ventilation in summer.*

Sunroom exterior *echoes design of original home down to last detail—from shingles to small-paned windows. Front of home faces west (gables are visible above addition's overhead glazing); south-facing sunroom is tucked behind garage.*

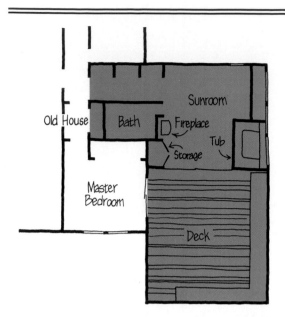

Gained: Room for relaxation, access to the outdoors

Adding a cozy study opens shady end of house to sun

New large deck adjoins both the added sunroom and the new master bedroom.

Brick fireplace, wood floor, rough fir walls and ceiling create "natural" feeling.

As an addition to a very old farmhouse, this pleasant room brings in the sun's light and warmth and provides a sense of openness as well as easy access to the outdoors.

All year around, the sunroom is at a comfortable temperature: a large oak tree and one wall of sliding glass doors keep it cool in summer. In winter, most of the heat comes from the sun through windows and acrylic skylights. The room has a wood-burning fireplace and electric heat if needed; when unoccupied it can be closed off from the rest of the house to save fuel.

The addition also includes a half bath and a sunken tub where the owners can soak and look out into the surrounding trees. Adjoining the sunroom is a new deck with built-in seating along two sides.

Building materials create attractive contrasts: Alaskan yellow cedar for the deck and benches, redwood for exterior walls, Douglas fir for interior walls and peaked ceiling, random-width white oak for the floor, earth-tone tiles around the sunken tub, and cedar lining for the closets.

Architect: Sandra Miller. Landscape designer: Michael Wills.

Abundance of windows, wood, ceramic tile, houseplants, casual furnishings help create feeling merging indoors and outdoors.

Once a solarium, now a family entertainment area

Materials salvaged from original house used in addition

This lovely old 1905 house had a more-than-ample formal living room for entertaining, but it lacked a good place for the family's four children and their friends to spend time (there are always lots of young people using the tennis court in the backyard). To keep tennis balls out of the living room, the owners expanded a small solarium into a large, informal rumpus room for the young set.

The finished room works well for the entire family. Both parents and children do a lot of entertaining; the adults in the living room and the young people in the rumpus room can enjoy privacy simultaneously.

The addition uses doors, beams, and shingles that retain the traditional character of the house. Carpenters saved as many materials as possible when they removed an exterior wall, and used them to finish off the new exterior. Inside, the beams from the ceiling of the adjoining living room are reiterated in the new room.

Architect: James Mount.

New rumpus room receives ample light

Rumpus room addition contains plenty of space for visiting with friends, bumper pool, and a relatively quiet game of chess.

TRANSFORMATIONS:
Gaining space with room conversions

When it seems the only solution to a lack of space is adding on, take a fresh look at the "rooms" in your house that aren't now being used as living spaces— the attic, basement, and garage. With a little imagination and work, these underutilized areas can be turned into bright, pleasant living spaces. And because these spaces are already sheltered, you'll spend far less money to convert them into comfortable, livable rooms than you would to build an addition.

Though you won't need to construct a roof, floor, or walls, you will have to address special concerns when converting a space not built for living into a room. For example, head room can be an issue in attics and some basements; in the attic especially, the roof may need to be re-engineered to provide enough vertical space. Basements, attics, and garages must be sealed against the weather; they may require insulation, caulking, and moistureproofing.

Since a maze of utility pipes, wires, and ducts often runs through these spaces, you'll need to either reroute them or design around them. You may also have to create proper access, especially in the case of an attic that's reachable only through a trap door or a basement with steep, narrow stairs.

Finally, you'll want to consider light. In the attic, you can add dormers or skylights; in the basement, you'll probably have to rely on artificial light.

Opening up roof ridge helped turn a dark attic into a bright work and play space; a 4 by 28-foot skylight runs along ridge, bringing light into entire area. Under dormer is a built-in work center; a couch and bookcase nestle in niche by stairway balustrade. Architect: Daniel Phipps, Phipps & Tritt.

A dark basement was transformed into this cheerful family room, complete with oak floors, recessed lighting, and built-in shelves and counters. Casement windows and French doors take advantage of only wall fully above grade. Architects: Peter Brock and Jack Hoyt.

Hillside home reaches down for room

"Daylight basement" becomes bright guest room and study

If you want to expand your house without adding on, one direction to look is down. Basements are fairly common in older houses, particularly in the East and Midwest. And hillside homes often have "daylight basements" — rooms with one side above ground and both ends partially exposed.

Here is the bold renovation of a house built in the early 1900s with a shallow basement and an open-air porch under the main floor.

By opening the basement to the porch and enclosing them as a single wide-open area, what had been storage space became a combination guest room and study with a generous view out to the garden. The absence of stairwells adds to the open feeling.

The old porch floor was replaced with brick laid in sand on the ground to drain excess water from plants. The hardwood floor of the main room, a foot higher, was laid over existing concrete.

The unusual shape of the two openings to the garden (one is a door, the other a window) follows the line of the house supports; fixed glass around the window and door allows maximum light to enter the room.

Architect: A. O. Bumgardner.

Imaginatively shaped entry helps draw the outdoors into this remodeled basement.

Pair of interesting shapes cuts stylish design in basement wall.

Glass-door garden entry to basement rooms

Stairway up
from basement

Open stairway descends into new
living area with its hardwood floor.
Entry floor, foreground, is brick.

900-square-foot farmhouse opens up

Newly enclosed back porch, plus built-ins, gains space

The decaying 1890s farmhouse had one important asset: it looked as though it belonged in its sleepy vineyard setting. Its raised front porch and front door flanked by double-hung windows powerfully evoked an earlier era.

Inside, it was a mess. Plumbing and appliances were primitive; you had to walk through the bathroom to get to the backyard. Most walls needed rebuilding, and closets were minimal.

To make the house habitable without obliterating its character, the architect decided to revamp the floor plan slightly and enclose a back porch for use as a master bedroom, bringing the finished interior space up to 1,296 square feet. He turned the old bathroom into a dining porch and converted one of the four original bedrooms to a new bathroom. Another bedroom was removed and the extra space added to the living room.

The two small remaining bedrooms needed storage space, so it was built in. The beds themselves serve as cabinets, bookcases, and night tables; built-in closets hold clothing.

In the living room, an interior window to the kitchen allows a glimpse of the space beyond, making both rooms seem larger than they are. A big new multipaned window in the kitchen doubles the amount of light brought in but respects the carpenter-built tradition of the original windows.

Architect: William Turnbull, William Turnbull Associates.

Built-ins *make the most of 8 by 12-foot bedroom. Bed is part of platform with storage cupboards at each end, trundle underneath.*

New interior window *by fireplace allows glimpse of kitchen, uncramping both small kitchen and living room and letting in light from new kitchen window.*

Left: Crisp outlines of front porch posts and trim accent old farmhouse's character; back porch has been enclosed to become a bedroom. ***Above:*** Big new kitchen window lets in cheerful sunshine; new fir cabinets and softwood flooring create a warm, homey atmosphere.

From old garage to new family room

A rainy-day retreat for the children

Sometimes you can add a room without adding more area to your house. The owners of this house did just that. They wanted more room for informal family activities and for dining off the kitchen area.

Once they decided that space for cars wasn't as important as space for people, they transformed half the garage into a new family room. There is still garage enough for a single car—as required by the local zoning ordinance.

The new room doesn't extend all the way out to the street-side wall; some former garage space was left to provide storage. Also, a new street-side window opens directly into the family room.

Separate yet easily observable from the kitchen, the new room provides an excellent retreat for the family's young children, and is a lifesaver on a rainy day. It allows the old family area adjacent to the kitchen to be used as a large informal dining area and gathering place for conversation or study.

Architects: Churchill-Zlatunich-Lorimer.

Family room has beamed ceiling, skylight, and track lighting. Low-maintenance tile floor adds informal tone.

Before

After

Cramped attic is now a comfortable studio/guest room

Lounge-niches accommodate overnight guests

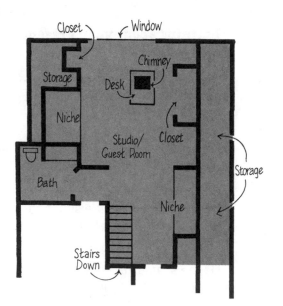

Once a cramped space under a sloping roof, this second-floor conversion is like getting an addition without adding any extra space. It has become a studio/guest room as airy and open as a tree house.

What opened things up was a full glass gable end wall overlooking the garden. Removing the dropped ceiling and adding new beams made a big difference, as did the two new sleeping or lounging niches.

The niches leave a maximum of floor space open and free of furniture in a narrow room where standing space under the roof slope measures only 12 feet across. The skylights above each niche help balance the light from the glass gable at the room's end; without them the room would resemble a tunnel.

To save more space, a work table surrounds the furnace chimney that ascends through the middle of the room. The chimney itself is sheathed in wood strips of varying thickness — a timbered version of flagstones.

Designer: Richard W. Painter.

Niches *for sitting and sleeping are built under sloping portion of roof. Above them, skylights let in daylight, night sky views.*

PLANNING GUIDELINES:
How to Get Started

Remodeling your house promises exciting transformations—more space, more light, a new feeling of openness. But these rewards are not easily gained; the remodeling process can be a long and disruptive experience. Depending on the scope of your project, you may spend weeks or months meeting with architects and contractors, dealing with work crews in and around your house, and taking care of an endless list of details.

To help you sort out the sometimes bewildering process of remodeling or adding on, we offer in this section a general outline of the procedures involved in planning and carrying out space-expanding projects.

DOING YOUR "HOMEWORK"

Before you start planning, try to pin down exactly what you want and need in terms of space. Get to know your house as it is now: study its structure as well as the way it works—or doesn't work—for living. The drawing on page 76 will help you understand terms you'll need to know.

Although much of this preliminary work isn't strictly necessary if you're going to turn over the design and/or construction to professionals, it can help you get a better idea of what you want before you talk to a professional.

Reviewing your needs and options

First, consider carefully the shortcomings of your present house. Is it dark, inefficient, or just plain too small? Perhaps the storage space is inadequate, or your family has outgrown the available bedrooms and baths. Or maybe you need space for recreational activities or for a home office.

Next, review all the possible options, trying to be as specific as possible. Your first decision will have to be whether you can reorder the space you already have, perhaps by converting an attic into a bedroom or by taking down walls, or whether you have to add on.

If you decide that only an addition will do the job, think about what uses it should serve. A new family room, for example, can do double-duty as a game room, a dining area, or even a guest room. Also consider the traffic patterns in the new room or rooms and the effect of the addition on traffic patterns throughout the rest of the house.

Think, too, about overall design. Some people want an addition to blend so completely with the existing house that there's no telling where one stops and the other begins. Others don't mind a contrasting addition, as long as it harmonizes with the existing structure. Still others prefer bold, new designs that share no simi-

larities whatever with the style of the existing house.

Learning about your present house

Once you have some general notions about what you want, gather all the pertinent information concerning the structure of your house. Depending on whether you're adding a room, converting an attic or basement, or opening up existing space, you'll need to know the structure and condition of the roof, walls, and foundation.

House structure. Find out which are the bearing walls (the ones that support the house). Any remodeling that involves removal of all or part of a bearing wall adds to the complexity and expense of the project. Go into the basement or crawl space and measure the width and depth of your foundation; if you'd like to add a second story, for example, your foundation must be able to support it, or you'll have to put in a new foundation. Take a look at the roof; it may require reinforcing if you want to remodel an attic or remove a ceiling.

Utilities. Try to determine where all the pipes are. If possible, trace them in the walls and under the floors; the farther away from existing plumbing a new bathroom or other room requiring plumbing fixtures is, the more complicated and expensive the installation will be.

If you're considering tearing down a wall or removing a ceiling, you'll also want to trace electrical wiring and heating and cooling ducts, since they may have to be rerouted.

Your lot. If you want to add on, measure your lot and the existing structures on it. Also measure the distances from the structures to the property lines and to the street. These can be all-important zoning considerations.

A scale drawing of your house can be very helpful when you're planning your remodeling.

Once you've gathered all the necessary information, collect it on a fact sheet for reference. You may want to make a scale drawing of your house, including utilities. The more thoroughly you understand the existing situation, the better prepared you'll be to deal with changes or additions.

WORKING WITH PROFESSIONALS

When you're ready to make some firm plans for your project, you'll need to decide to what extent you want to involve professionals and how much you want to do yourself.

Professionals you may be working with on a remodeling project include an architect or designer, a contractor, and various subcontractors, such as a plumber and an electrician. Unless you're designing and constructing the entire project yourself, your level of involvement with these professionals can vary widely, from simply calling someone in occasionally to turning the entire job over to them from start to finish.

Whatever route you take, it's a good idea to consult a professional early in the planning stage to get a ballpark figure of the cost and to explore generally the feasibility of your ideas.

CONSULTING AN ARCHITECT OR DESIGNER

An architect is a licensed professional whose training includes education in design from the esthetic, functional, and engineering points of view. To get a license, an architect must pass a rigorous examination. A designer isn't licensed. Either design professional may consult with a structural engineer on some projects.

Your architect or designer may design the project, provide working drawings and specifications, and then leave the construction and its supervision up to you. Or, the architect or designer can do everything from designing through monitoring construction. Some design professionals don't like to "let go" of their work before it's fully completed; they like to make certain that their designs are correctly realized by the builder. Obviously, contract administration by a design professional removes a big burden from the homeowner, but it also increases the bill.

To find an architect or designer, consult with friends or neighbors who have worked with such professionals. You can also call the nearest office of the American Institute of Architects or the nearest office of the American Institute of Building Designers, though not all practicing architects and designers belong to these organizations. Real estate brokers may be helpful.

Once you've located some architects or designers, you can arrange a meeting with each one to discuss your plans and needs, and to look at some of the professional's building plans and photos of finished projects. Ask for the names and addresses of other clients that you can call. Be strong in expressing your concern for a good working relationship, and in general try to determine whether you'd be happy working with the person. Because remodeling your home is a personal project, you'll want an architect or designer who not only is technically and artistically skilled, but also is someone with whom you feel comfortable.

After you've done some shopping, think things over carefully and make your choice. Once you've agreed to employ a particular architect or designer, the next meeting should be in your home, where the planning will begin. Be sure to make known from the very beginning your budget for this part of the remodel. Then you and the architect or designer can sit down and work out a payment method, which can range from an hourly fee to a percentage of the entire project's cost.

CONSULTING A CONTRACTOR

A general contractor is a licensed professional builder whose responsibility is the actual building of a structure. Many contractors can also design (or help you design) a project. To do the building, contractors normally employ carpenters and arrange for other work, such as plumbing and wiring, to be done by subcontractors on a project-by-project basis.

Since your contractor is such an important part of the building process, it's very important that you find a person with whom you can have a good working relationship. If your architect is monitoring the construction of your project, he or she will be instrumental in hiring the general con-

tractor (subject, of course, to your approval). But if you're supervising the work, you'll have to find the contractor yourself.

Choosing a contractor

You can get the names of contractors from architects and designers, from friends, from trade associations, or from material suppliers. Call the contractors whose names you've collected and ask for several references; then talk to those clients about the contractors and arrange to see their work, both from the outside and the inside.

On the basis of that procedure, select two or three promising contractors. Ask them for names of material suppliers and subcontractors and bank and credit references; check these to learn the financial condition of the firm.

Contractors are accustomed to providing such information and should give you these references willingly. You can also call your local Better Business Bureau to find out if there have been any complaints filed against a contractor.

In addition, verify the validity of contractors' licenses with the state licensing agency and check their public liability and property damage and workers' compensation insurance with their insurance carriers.

Submit your plans and specifications to two or three contractors for bids. The list of specifications should be as detailed as possible, including all materials, appliance model numbers, types of fixtures, paints and stains, and so forth.

You don't have to choose the least expensive bid. In some

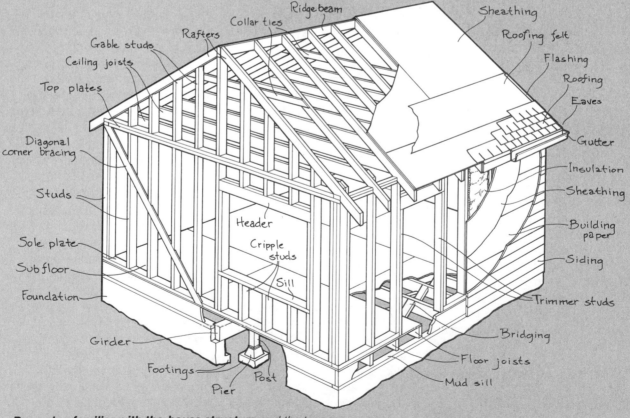

Becoming familiar with the house structure *and the terms used to describe it will help you deal with both the planning and professionals during remodeling stages.*

cases, it may be worth it to pay more for certain pluses, such as higher-quality workmanship or a more amicable relationship with the contractor. Even so, bids are the chief consideration for most homeowners.

Drawing up a contract

Once you've accepted a bid, you and the contractor will draw up a written contract based on that bid. As the working agreement between you and your contractor, the contract is a very important document—you can refer to it if any differences arise. Therefore, it's important to make the contract as detailed as possible.

Construction materials. The contract should list all materials to be used in construction. It should be thoroughly detailed, itemizing all materials and fixtures, even things that may seem insignificant, such as drawer pulls and cabinet hinges. If any disagreements arise about materials, you and your contractor can refer to this list of agreed-upon specifications. Anything not included in the contract and added later will increase your cost.

Time schedule. You and your contractor may include in the contract a time schedule for the project—a beginning date and a completion date. The contractor obviously can't be responsible for delays caused by strikes or material shortages, and you have no effective legal way to enforce a schedule even though it's written into the contract. Your best leverage is a good working relationship with the contractor—and the stipulation that the final payment will be withheld until the work is completed.

Site preparation and cleanup. If you're adding on, your building

site may need to be prepared for construction: fences and shrubs removed, concrete torn up, land graded. If you expect the contractor to do this, be sure to include it in the contract.

As a job progresses, and once it's finished, there will be a lot of debris on the site, and disposing of it usually is no easy matter. Again, if you expect the contractor to clean up, it must be in the contract.

Method of payment. Payment, of course, is covered in the contract as well. Usually, payment is made in installments as the work progresses, or with an initial payment at the beginning of the project and the balance at the project's completion. You should withhold the final payment until after the lien period has expired and until the certificate of completion has been issued by your local building department. If you have secured outside financing, the financing agency may hold its final payment until the lien period has expired.

Protection against liens. Under the laws of most states, people who perform labor or supply materials for a building can file a lien against the building if they are not paid. If the contractor doesn't settle the claim, the building's owner may be liable.

There are various ways to protect yourself against this eventuality: you can pay suppliers of material and labor directly; you can require evidence of such payment from the contractor before making each progress payment and the final payment; or you can require the contractor to post a bond of sufficient size specifically to protect your property. This bond would be in addition to the one required by the state from a licensed contractor—that minimum bond might

not be large enough to cover all claims against a contractor.

To be valid, liens must be filed within a specified time after construction is completed, and the time limit that a lien remains in effect is also specified by law. If you are selling your property during this period, the settlement of valid liens by payment or legal action will be required before title is transferred.

The laws covering liens vary from state to state, so you should consult an attorney before entering into any contract for work on your property.

Working with a contractor

In the course of a remodeling project, it's normal for problems to arise. Don't be dismayed by disagreements you might have with your contractor. Clearly, you have a personal attachment to the project not shared by your contractor.

Once the project gets going, keep a close eye on the work and the materials being used. Feel free to ask questions—it's your house and your money—but try not to get in the way of the work. And you should try to be around home at least some part of every day so the contractor can ask you questions. Don't give direct instructions to the contractor's employees or to subcontractors; always deal directly with the contractor.

After the job is completed, you should address a formal letter of acceptance to the contractor, who then files a completion notice with the county recorder's office.

If you plan to hire a contractor but want to do some of the work yourself, be sure your contractor agrees to this arrangement. Some of the most common jobs homeowners do during construction include installing insulation, painting, and cleaning up. Your contractor will want to be assured that your part in the work won't delay completion of the job. Your responsibilities will be spelled out in the contract, and you'll have to sign a written statement releasing the contractor from any liability for the work you perform.

And, of course, your contract may call for the contractor to do only a limited amount of work—the foundation, frame, and roof of an addition, for instance. Once that is done and the contractor has left the job, you can finish the project yourself.

ACTING AS YOUR OWN CONTRACTOR

Being your own general contractor means that you will be responsible for everything from obtaining permits to hiring subcontractors to arranging for building inspections. But before you do anything else, check with your insurance broker. Your standard homeowner's policy will *not* cover liability for injury to persons you employ for construction. It's a simple matter, but a major expense, for you to purchase a policy, known as workers' compensation insurance, to cover your liability for work-related injuries.

When you put various parts of your project out to bid with subcontractors, you must use the same care you'd exercise in hiring a general contractor. You will need to check references, financial resources, and insurance coverage of a number of subcontractors, get bids, work out detailed contracts, and then carefully supervise the work. The process will be time-consuming,

but you'll save money and have more control over the quality of the work.

ZONING ORDINANCES AND BUILDING CODES

Every community has zoning ordinances and building codes to protect standards of health, safety, and land use. Remodeling done to your house must comply with these standards. Compliance is monitored in two ways: your building plans must be approved by officials before you can begin work, and the work in progress will be inspected periodically.

If you hire an architect or designer to design your project and a general contractor to build it, you may never come in contact with the building inspector or the planning commission—except, perhaps, to make some inquiries in the preliminary planning stages. The professionals working for you will take care of satisfying all zoning and code requirements and getting all necessary permits and inspections. If, on the other hand, you do all the work yourself, you will need to deal directly with the building department and the planning office.

Even if you plan to have everything done by professionals, familiarizing yourself with zoning restrictions and building codes can help you in the early planning stages, before you call in the architect or contractor. If you take rough plans to a building inspector, you can find out whether they violate building ordinances or codes, and, if they do, you can ask for some suggestions about how to bring them into conformity.

Zoning ordinances. Designed to regulate community land use, zoning ordinances, which can vary widely from community to community, may affect your proposed remodel. In general, they separate commercial, industrial, and residential areas, establishing boundaries to prevent business from migrating into residential neighborhoods.

Zoning ordinances regulate land use *within* each area, too. Regulations apply largely to the exterior and location of structures, but they also apply to the way the property is used, such as for business purposes. Sections of the zoning ordinances pertaining to residential zones may regulate the following:

• Occupancy—the number of persons unrelated by blood or marriage who may live in a dwelling.
• Commercial use—the types of businesses allowed.
• Height of buildings.
• Distances between structure and property lines.
• Percentage of lot covered by structure.
• Parking requirements.
• Architectural style.

Additions and zoning ordinances. Here are several questions relating to zoning ordinances that you should consider if you're planning an addition:

• Will the house with the addition occupy a greater percentage of the lot than is permitted under the ordinance?
• Will the boundary wall of the addition come closer to the side lot boundary than the permitted distance?
• If the addition involves adding a second story, will it extend the roof crest above the height limit for your zone?
• Are you required to have covered, off-street parking?

• Will an addition to the front of the house come too close to the street-side property line? One of the most common miscalculations homeowners make is to consider the front sidewalk as the street boundary of their property. In many communities, the front property line is actually a few feet back from the sidewalk. Before you launch a project that involves adding on to the front of the house, check your plot plan—available at the tax assessor's office—to find out just where your street-side boundary actually runs.

If your proposed addition violates the zoning ordinance and you have a good reason for wishing to deviate from zoning requirements, you may apply for a variance, but to get it you'll need to prove that strict application of the rules would result in "practical difficulties or undue hardship." If your addition is being professionally designed, your architect or designer will work with you throughout the variance process.

An approved variance is usually valid for 1 year. If you haven't completed the addition within that time, you must reapply. However, building inspectors can certify that work is in progress and extend the deadline.

Building codes. Building codes are concerned principally with construction practices—structural design and strength and durability of building materials. The codes state what you can and cannot do in erecting a structure. For example, codes regulate the square footage of bedrooms, the area of windows in habitable rooms, and similar matters. In addition, they regulate specifications for foundations, framing, electrical wiring, and plumbing.

Properly enforced, building codes ensure that steel is actually inside the foundations, that spans are within limits so floors won't sag, that walls are properly braced and nailed, and so on. Usually, you can obtain excerpts of the regulations that apply to your particular situation from the building department.

In some situations, particularly if you're adding on to an older home, strict application of the building code could require you to bring the entire house up to the present code. This is almost always the case if the cost of the addition totals more than 50 percent of the present market value of the house, excluding the lot.

If a proposed remodel or addition doesn't conform to the building code, it may still be approved. The head of the building department has the authority to permit suitable alternatives, provided they do not weaken the structure, endanger the safety or security of the occupants, or violate the property rights of neighbors.

In some instances, the plans for your proposed project might require review by a licensed structural engineer. This normally happens when the design is unusual and the building inspector or other official feels that it warrants closer scrutiny.

SHOPPING FOR FINANCING

If you're embarking on a major project, such as adding on to your house, you'll finance your addition by arranging some kind of loan. But before making any loan arrangements, you must have finished plans and specifications for your project and accurate estimates. If you plan to do the work yourself, go to suppliers to establish the costs of all materials; otherwise, your contractor will supply this information. Next, you need to determine the type of financing that best suits your needs and for which you can qualify.

The type of financing that's best depends primarily on how much money you need to borrow. You'll need to research the various types of loans available in your area to learn their terms, since these vary widely from one lending institution to another. You can borrow for home improvements from a variety of sources: commercial banks, savings and loan associations, savings banks, mortgage banks, and credit unions.

Once you have a general idea how the terms of various loans relate to your personal financial situation, you can approach lending institutions. Start with a lender where you've done business before, such as a bank where you have a savings or checking account, or a credit union where you've financed a car. Your past or present business there may be just the right foundation for a new home improvement loan.

You may also be able to finance your project by borrowing against your life insurance equity, refinancing your present mortgage, obtaining a second mortgage, or remortgaging your home if it is paid for. Check the details of these methods as they pertain to your situation.

To obtain a loan, you'll need to file an application with a lending institution, stating the purpose of the loan and the amount needed. You'll also have to provide personal financial data that will convince the lender the loan is a good risk. Make sure your credit record is in order first.

Sunset
Proof-of-Purchase
ISBN 0-376-01366-4

INDEX

Photographers

Glenn Allison: 56 (right). **Glenn
Christiansen:** 47, 48, 49, 50, 55, 57, 71.
Mark Citret: 30. **Stephen Cridlan:** 11.
Jack McDowell: 4, 5, 6, 12, 13, 14, 19,
28, 29, 42, 58, 64, 65, 66, 72. **Don
Normark:** 22. **Norman A. Plate:** 27, 56
(left). **David Stubbs:** 41. **Rob Super:** 20,
21. **Tom Wyatt:** 63.